How to Become a Witch

An Essential Introductory Guide to the Wiccan Religion, Important Wiccan Beliefs and Rituals, and How to Cast Spells that Work

by Elsey Willows

Table of Contents

Introduction

Before we start, let's guide your thoughts along a framework more conducive to understanding the journey upon which you're about to embark. Wicca is not a religion in the modern sense – as that word has been defined by the Abrahamic religions. But rather, it is a religion as the Ancients understood the word – a path of spirituality which brings you closer to the divine energy all around us, and which helps you fulfill your own potential as a sentient being through compassion, love, and acceptance.

Wicca is an experiential journey – there is no right or wrong answer, and what you believe at the end of your current lifespan may not even be what you believed when you first embarked upon it. The only thing that guides you is the fruit of your own experiences, as you strive to find the path which resonates strongest with your soul.

Let me try and explain in another way: Have you ever gotten your dream job? Or felt like you found your soul-mate? Or have you experienced a piece of music which spoke to you at the deepest level of your soul? In any of these moments that may have moved you, personally or professionally, did you feel an uplifting sensation rise from the bottom of your toes to the top of your scalp? Or even a body-wide tingling which made you feel more joyous or emotional than ever before? Did you feel an undeniable sense of *rightness* in the situation? That's what I mean by *resonance* of the soul. As confusing and chaotic as life may be, the divine often gives us a tangible or palpable signal – that can't be ignored – telling us that we are on the right path. This feeling, this divine sensation, is what guides one's choices in Wicca. Beyond a few important rules and guidelines, everything that determines your own path along life's journey is in your hands alone. Wicca is simply a way of getting in touch with your inner-self, and celebrating your life and place in that oldest form of the Divine – the universal balance of natural energy.

Also – there is no singular *set form of Wicca*. If someone has ever told you that Wicca *should* be this way or that, then they have entirely missed the point of this experience (unfortunately, that happens even with people who have been Wiccans for most of their lives). Wicca is an experiential, subjective experience which is defined by **your** beliefs. Therefore, I'm not going to teach you **my** Wiccan beliefs or **my** path in this guide. All I'm going to do is to outline what Wicca is, and how can you find **your own** spiritual path. I'll go over the basic tools you'll need, and how can you cast your own spells. I'll also discuss everything from choosing your own God and

Goddess to whom you wish to dedicate your worship, and how to select your mystical name. In the end, I'll provide you with the framework – the entire structure – which you need to discover your own Wiccan self, and how you choose to proceed with it beyond that point will be left entirely up to you. Because **that** is the true essence of Wicca – the freedom of beliefs in the search of the divine, and love and acceptance of your brothers and sisters, come what may. (And just to be clear, the name 'witch' is unisex and applies to both men and women.)

Before we begin – I invoke the benevolent Moon Goddess and the passionate Sun God, and request them to grant you compassion, wisdom, strength and clarity as you take your first steps into this exciting journey. May you always find love and support, and spread tolerance and warmth to others through your cosmic radiance. Let's get started!

Chapter 1: Common Misconceptions about Wicca

While many authors like to deal with misconceptions at the end of their literary works, I've often found it best to clear the air right as one steps through a new door. If people approach any new topic through a haze of ill-conceived notions, I have found that it often taints their primary impressions and leaves them with far less clarity than if those subjects had been dealt with right at the beginning.

Also, while I'm sure that there are many other misconceptions in addition to the ones I chose to answer here, I tried to address the ones that I've seen plague newcomers most often.

[1] Wicca, Paganism, Satanism, Mysticism

The biggest misconception that I've noticed people have is that Wicca is somehow linked to devil worship, or is somehow linked to the arts of Black Magic. Nothing could be further from the truth. Wicca is the worship of the energies in nature, and celebrates life itself. We believe that the most primordial form of the divine was simply that – energy. Out of that energy came the Gods and Goddesses, regardless of ethnicity or religious background. While there are tricksters and evil entities in nature as well, there is no Devil or Satan – that being an Abrahamic construct (Islam, Judaism, Christianity). Without intending to dredge up any negative sentiments, a significant portion of these misconceptions came through the persecution of Wiccans by monotheistic religions in the Middle and Dark ages, in an attempt to establish their dominance over older spiritual paths and thus enhance their own political legitimacy. In fact, the descriptions of the horned Satan – half man, half goat, with horns on his head – used by Abrahamics in their dark-age persecution is a direct description of the Greek God Pan, God of the Wilds and Nature. He is the ruler of wild places and is known for his virility. The Pan flute – made of reed pipes – is named after him. Does that sound "devil"ish to you?

Wicca is called a pagan religion by many, but *pagan* (paganus) was a derogatory term used by Roman Christians for rural people who refused to let go of their older paths of spirituality instead of embracing Christianity. *Paganism* again is therefore an Abrahamic construct. Using that term to classify Wicca is not only insulting, but rather like debating whether the footwear worn by Martian aliens is more similar to Nike or Air Jordans (as an example; reductio ad absurdum). It's a rather narrow-minded attempt to understand someone else's set of beliefs through the framework created by an ignorant and unappreciative outsider, rather than try and approach its understanding through your own eyes, and derive your own conclusions. To be accurate, Wicca is a nature-based religion.

Mysticism means the belief in mystical energies which are ever-present around beings in nature, and such spiritual paths often have rituals and rites which seek to use those mystical energies in a specific manner as directed by the will of the user. In such a framework, Wicca is a mystical religion, and a very ancient one at that – having been around in its skeletal form for millennia, and was first brought over to the States through British mysticism and Druidic religions several centuries ago. It was introduced in a semblance of its current form in the U.S mainstream in the mid-1900s. As a comparison, mysticism does not mean the negative manipulation of spell-casting – another world-famous mystic religion being Tantric or Tibetan Buddhism, accompanied by several schools of Taoism, or Zen spirituality.

[2] Is Wicca a Feminist Religion?

As funny as this may sound, I've actually faced this question many times from newcomers and outsiders in my long experience as a Wiccan. Wicca believes in balance – and therefore each coven (a group of three to thirteen practitioners often led by a High Priest (HP) and High Priestess (HPS)), usually dedicates their worship to a God as well as Goddess. In Wicca, energy and life are pointless without balance – yin is incomplete without yang, female energy is incomplete without the male (energy and gender aren't the same thing here; some males have more female energy, and vice versa).

The unfortunate truth is that, since Wicca was one of the only spiritual paths which emphasized the female nature of the Divine just as much as the male, it gained a significant feminist following who regrettably used their spiritual path as an outlet for their political frustrations. It's not uncommon to hear of some covens who treat their male members rather brashly, or outright disrespectfully. However, that is the failing of the *coven* to understand the true meaning of Wicca and to let their mundane frustrations color their experience of the Divine, rather than the other way round. If you're a male Wiccan, and you come across such a coven, move on! Wicca is a religion that celebrates and needs masculinity just as much as femininity, and so welcomes men and women alike with open arms. One of the larger growing problems because of such petty covens today is that there are far fewer males than are needed to achieve balance in our covens, and so Wicca is suffering from a lack of equal masculine perspective in its practice – a problem which I hope this guide will help correct in some part.

[3] Wicca and Magic

When most people hear magic, they think *Harry Potter* or *Game of Thrones* (That's right, Wiccans watch HBO too). With some exceptions in the latter series, Wiccan magic could not be further from pop culture's current understanding of the term. As I mentioned earlier, Wiccans believe in natural energy. Therefore, we are born, we die, we exist as energy, and at some point we will be reborn – either as a plant, animal, human, etc. Regardless, natural energy keeps going around in a constant cycle of life and death, and it exists all around us – which is how life is sustained. Wiccans believe that sentient beings can, and always have been able to, tap into those energy resources and use their will to shape that external energy into achieving a definite outcome. This isn't something that only a chosen few can perform, and skill and talent have no part to play in the process.

Wiccan magic is a result of intense study, research and dedication to your craft, with practitioners spending year after year gaining a deeper understanding of their chosen deities and the various mechanics through which life may be *nudged* into gaining more favorable outcomes. It is a result of intense experimentation and failures, and some people spend decades writing and compiling a comprehensive repertoire of spells – the mechanics of which we shall discuss in further chapters.

[4] Can People Harm Me through Wicca?

While I did mention that Wicca is subjective and that there are varying degrees of light and dark in practitioners depending on their understanding of it – Wicca also has a few basic rules that give it form and structure, what little it may have. One of these basic laws is sanctity of the natural order in life. While there are many paths in Ancient Religions which do lead to darker avenues of spellcraft, Wicca is a path of *good* – as loosely as that term may be used in conjunction with nature.

If someone claims to be able to do harm through spellcraft, they're no longer Wiccan, and have descended into darker paths. Spellcraft in Wicca is intended to exert a positive influence on life, without any overwhelmingly negative influence in the life of someone else. For example, if you use a spell for luck in lottery, your win would raise your prosperity but it wouldn't *reduce* someone else's state of life – it would simply not budge from its previous status quo. Nor would it stop them from winning the next lottery, if it is so ordained through their luck. Moreover, this is a rather extreme example to enhance clarity – most Wiccan spells have less to do with a practitioner's relations with the outside world, and more to do with their own sense of well-being, their relationship with the divine, or their relationship with themselves and their environment.

The same applies to people who sell love spells and their ilk, they're no longer true Wiccans, but are opportunists who have descended into shameless profiteering by exploiting their very belief system. Such people have already started to distance their ties with the divine, and will soon lose much of their accumulated energies from their deities as a result. This is why Wiccans don't need supervisors or policing, because practitioners who break the basic rules and walk along darker paths cannot be punished worse than through the misfortunes which they ultimately bring upon themselves through their own harmful deeds.

[5] Can Wiccans Eat Meat?

Yes, we're Wiccans, not Vegans. There's a crucial difference there. Wicca is a nature-based religion, and so believes in the natural order of things – one of the most crucial parts of which is the food chain. There are many Wiccans who *choose* to not partake in meat, but that's a personal choice, not a religious one.

Wicca shuns *undue* harm of others, but the consumption of meat isn't *unduly* harmful. The energy you get from the meal is then used to fulfill your daily duties, your responsibilities to yourself, your family, and your productive contributions to society at large – either through your profession or other efforts. It respects the natural order, and converts the energy received through the meal into a positive force. Besides, plants have the same energy as well, so one way or another you're deriving that energy from a living being. Attacking an animal or person for petty causes, or perverse satisfaction goes against the laws of Wicca, and so does undue violence. However, as an example, if someone is physically threatening you or others, Wicca doesn't stop you from unleashing a can of butt whooping in self-defense.

[6] Are Wiccans Hippies?

This is the most absurd misconception created through B-grade pop culture about Wicca. Wiccans aren't layabouts or goths. They come from all walks and professions of life – doctors, nurses, lawyers, authors, cops, bankers, teachers, engineers, firemen, and other pillars of society – and many of whom I've known are quite highly respected in their communities for their professional achievements. You don't have to dress up as a sad vampire wannabe to be a Wiccan, and beyond certain ritualistic choices on specific days, there is no required dress code to be one.

In fact, with rising awareness about personal rights in the U.S, more Wiccans are choosing to come out of their closet each year since neither the law nor your professional establishment can isolate or bully you for your religious choices.

[7] Can Wiccans Celebrate Other Religions?

Yes. As I mentioned, Wicca is a spiritual path in which practitioners dedicate themselves to diverse gods and goddesses. If you're the follower of another religious path as well, as long as your own understanding of your religion allows you to reconcile this fact, Wicca is used by many to enhance their spiritual and religious experiences – and not supplant them. Of course, while many people just follow the path of Wicca, there are many practitioners who choose to reconcile between Abrahamic, older mystic, and other existential religions as well (just as there are many Christians today who choose to follow Buddhism as well, without needing to make a choice between one and the other). The restrictions against following Wicca never come from *inside* Wicca, but rather surrounding social or religious structures that prohibit practitioners from following this path or force them to make a choice.

I believe these answers should cover most of the common misconceptions about Wicca in your minds, so that we may approach the following chapters through a united discourse of tolerance and open-mindedness. With this out of the way, let's move on to the crux of our discussions.

Chapter 2: The Fundamentals of Wiccan Beliefs

As you may have gathered from my earlier statements, Wiccans believe in natural energy and the balance of forces. As per Wiccan beliefs, the oldest primordial force in nature is Energy. This energy had two major components – the male and the female. Therefore, when this energy took physical form, it resulted in Gods and Goddesses. In accordance with Wiccan belief, religion was always a very subjective experience for sentient beings and so the Gods and Goddesses who rose in different cultures were different in name, mythology, personality, etc. but were quite similar all the same. It was as if each God or Goddess were a different facet or aspect of that over-arching Energy. These Gods and Goddesses form two large entities – The Triple Goddess and The Horned God. Before you start wondering about the God, I need to reiterate that this isn't satanism. Horns were always revered as a sign of masculinity and virility, long before the religious persecution by the Abrahamics. The Horned God is the singular description of the various male gods who combine in their multitude of aspects to form the over-arching Masculine energy in nature.

The Triple Goddess is called so because she is the complete aspect of femininity, and thus carries within her reflections of the three major phases in the life of feminine energy – the Maiden, the Mother, and the Crone. Since Wiccans believe that life is a continuous cycle through the stream of Energy, this belief is reflected in the aspects of divinity.

The Maiden isn't a reference to *virginity* per se, but rather to the innocence of youth. The Maiden also symbolizes vitality, curiosity and independence.

The Mother is the second aspect of the feminine energy, and symbolizes nurturing, fertility, abundance, sexual and emotional fulfillment, and the gaining of experience and wisdom. Wiccans who celebrate the aspect of the Mother in their choice of Goddess do not have to become biological parents to embody these characteristics, but rather these qualities fulfill the role if embraced by themselves within one's attributes.

The final aspect of the Triple Goddess, and usually the most misunderstood one, is that of the Crone. In pop culture, the Crone is often portrayed as a negative and dark element, yet the qualities embodied by this aspect are wisdom, reverence, acceptance, and guidance to the next phase after Death. The qualities of the Crone aren't age or negativity, but rather to be wise and accepting of the last phase of the current lifespan before being spun through the cycle of Energy once again, and thus using the acceptance of one's limited time left to enjoy the current lifespan to the fullest. It is a fulfillment of one's responsibilities to oneself and one's younger generations, while living a positive and celebrated life without denying the prospect of the upcoming reset-button of Death in one's life.

The Horned God, as must be obvious by now, is the embodiment of all male aspects of the universal energy. The various aspects of the Horned God embody passion, virility, strength, roles of the protector and warrior, the just and wise, the hunter, the Lord of forest and field, and of sacrifice. Also called Cernunnos (Horned One), or even the Green Man, the God aspect is Lord of Light as well as Lord of Darkness, of Life, Death as well as Resurrection.

Finally, since every divine entity was birthed from the same source of Energy, which created all living things, every living organism is also birthed from that same Energy. Since we're all birthed from the same energy, the path to gain contact with the divine lies in each of us – and so we're our own priests and priestesses and do not rely on anyone else to form our subjective perception of the Divine. However, covens and groups may have more experienced members who lead through the offices of HPs and HPSs. A proper

HP or HPS' job is not to tell you what you believe, but rather to help you get closer to attaining your beliefs through knowledge and experience of proper ritualistic, mythological and spell-casting crafts.

With me so far? Good, because here's where the true scope of Wicca sucker-punches your expectations. While this is the basic structure of Wiccan belief, the God and Goddess mentioned here is the major cumulative form of all the aspects of the divine energy. While there are plenty of Wiccans who choose to worship the God and the Goddess as complete entities, there are many more who choose to dedicate themselves to specific aspects of the divine energy.

The Gods and Goddesses who are most commonly worshiped are the Celtic deities, the Greco-Roman Pantheon, the Egyptian deities, the Nordic Gods, as well as deities from other specific cultures or religions such as Mother Kali (Kali Ma) from Hinduism, etc. These don't even have to be the only Gods and Goddesses which Wiccans may choose from, some of them even opting to dedicate themselves to elemental spirits or totemic animal spirits from Native American mythology. As I mentioned before, Wiccan spirituality is the search for and dedication to a higher power which makes your soul resonate with a sense of *rightness*. In order to do so, Wiccans – whether they choose to join a like-minded coven or practice on their own – spend *at least* their first year studying and researching various Gods and Goddesses if they wish to dedicate themselves to a deity more specific in personality than the Triple Goddess or the Horned One. This is also the reason why many Wiccans wait a whole year before choosing their own mystical name as well – in case they wish to choose a name which gives tribute to their chosen deity.

The Creation Myth – a necessary part of the religious experience for many Wiccans – is also then derived from the mythology of the chosen God or Goddess. In fact, many Wiccans do the opposite as well – researching the thousands of creation myths in the rich cultural expanse of the human experience till they find one that personally appeals to them, and then choosing a God or Goddess from within the pantheon of the chosen culture.

Chapter 3: The Rules of Wicca

I'm sure that this fact must be getting clearer to you with every passing page you read – Wicca has no single doctrine or codified set of beliefs. Nowhere else is this more obvious than its rules. Put simply, there are no rules which apply to Wiccan practitioners all over the world except one – Do not cause harm to others (the limits and meaning of which we've already discussed before).

Beyond this, there are rules which a coven may choose to follow – but more so for unification of practice and etiquette than any religious necessity. In order to explain this further, let's quickly discuss the meaning of a coven.

Now, thanks to shows such as American Horror Story, people have a more ridiculous idea of covens than ever before. Covens aren't groups of male and female witches (male witches aren't called warlocks, which means oath breaker and is considered a derogatory term – though that may differ between covens) planning to overthrow the existing social order, while debating their choices of virginal sacrifices every evening over a fine glass of wine served by an immortal/brainwashed manservant. In its simplest terms, a coven can be equated to a book club – though much more serious, of course (unless your book club is really weird, or a secret Masonic front). By this analogy, I mean – if you're a lover of classic literature, would you want to join a book club which concentrates specifically on fantasy/fiction works? No, you wouldn't. It wouldn't meet your most basic needs and criteria, nor would you have any reason to invest your time and energy into it.

A coven is a group of three to thirteen (could be more or less, but both of these are mystical numbers and believed to hold power) people who wish to worship a common God or Goddess and thus advance their religious experiences among like-minded people with similar outlooks on spirituality, and the methods to go about it. Accordingly, each coven operates under its own sets of rules, and has its own system of initiation (some have it, some don't). A well-organized coven which meets your criteria will form your most stable social support system outside of your family and oldest friends. Your coven mates will be close to you for life, bonded as you are through common experiences, and will often give you support as and when needed in the outside world (one coven mate I knew was another's sponsor in AA, another opened two coven mates to professional prospects after they lost their jobs post-2008). This is why covens are particularly careful about who they choose to let in, and decide on their own codes of conduct.

One thing I need to reiterate – if you're a male Wiccan and you face a grand coven that treats you disrespectfully, leave! Sometimes, some Wiccans have the misfortune to join seemingly grand covens that treat them badly simply because they know of no other groups in their area. In such cases, it's far better to practice on your own than to compromise your self-respect. A coven exists to uplift its members, but some of them simply consist of HPs and HPSs on power trips who like treating other members like their slaves or retinue. I've already outlined the duties of a proper HP or HPS, and it is vital to keep that in mind while looking for a coven to join. Ideally, a good coven is for life, or at least a significant portion of your future – barring any moves or other life events which necessitate joining a new one. However, before joining a coven, keep in mind that you're making a solemn commitment to a supportive religious body – it's not a frat house – you need to figure out beforehand if you'll be able to make the necessary time commitments needed to devote yourself to the coven's activities, or if it would be better to simply practice on your own.

Beyond the specific rules of each coven, there are other rules which are specific to rituals and ceremonies, and which you'll pick up or be informed of as you go along by other members around you. Chief among them is that – while there is a certain amount of alcohol which is used in some rituals, abuse of any substance or consumption of drugs is frowned upon. Although some people legally choose to indulge in Marijuana, that is a personal recreational act and has nothing to do with worship – regardless of what others may tell you. In fact, if someone tries to get you to consume an intoxicant by telling you that it's for ritualistic purposes, you may want to get out and reconsider the validity of your choice in practicing partners!

Beyond these rules, there are also other frameworks which were created and which are followed by many covens – chief among which is the Wiccan Rede. This was the product of Gardnerian Wicca, and a creation of its founder. It was proposed as a moral ethos, rather than a set of rules or guidelines, and is the yardstick by which many Witches have chosen to regulate their conduct and practice. However, structure in practice helps in focusing your energies, and so if any of you wish to follow the creeds of the Wiccan Rede, a simple search on Google should be sufficient to lead you to several sources for the full version.

Expounding upon the rule to not harm others, Wiccans also strictly follow the Three-fold Law (or Law of Three), particularly when it comes to working magic. This law states that whatever energy you put out into the world, whether positive or negative, will come back at you three-fold. This is one that you always need to respect once you start dabbling in spellcraft, since the destructive effects of negative energy won't be visible in some distant lifetime or an absent afterlife, but in your near to distant future and may not only affect you alone but others around you whom you love or hold dear as well. Such is the law of nature.

A further point to mention here isn't a rule or law, but is universally followed nonetheless. Before one attempts to evoke a deity, or even hold a ritual or spell, one needs to purify him/herself physically and spiritually. This is to ensure that negative energies don't cross over into your attempts and thus result in either failed or distorted efforts. This particular practice is held sacred between all serious Wiccan practitioners, since a witch's spiritual practices aren't just a religious affiliation to some denomination, but an everyday ever-present vital aspect of our lives.

A last point to mention here is similarly a matter of etiquette – never ever touch someone else's ritualistic tools. Similarly, never ever let someone else touch your tools and paraphernalia of your craft. Understanding Wicca as a religion of energy, we, its practitioners, strongly believe that we imbue our own essence and energy into each tool we use – which accounts for the successes and failures having a strong affinity to the tools' owner. Thus breaking this barrier is the worst possible violation of our sacred boundaries.

Chapter 4: Understanding the Wheel of the Year

Since Wiccans celebrate the Sun as well as Moon deities, they follow both solar and lunar calendars. Arising from the fact that Wicca is an ancient nature-based religion, the largest celebrations in the Wiccan calendar are seasonal as well as agricultural. The Wiccan calendar itself is called "The Wheel of the Year" with eight major celebrations marking times of great change which are called Sabbats. These days mark solar phases and represent the ever-continuing cycle of birth, life, death and rebirth.

Apart from the Sabbat, the celebrations of the Moon Goddess at the height of her power are called Esbats. These are held 13 times in a year, once at each full moon.

The eight great Sabbats are the following:

Samhain: This is the Witch's New Year and is situated between the Autumn Equinox and Winter Solstice. Typically celebrated around the end of October/beginning of November, Samhain is the day at which the veil between life and death is at its thinnest. Wiccans believe that this is the day when the God dies and waits for his rebirth at Yule. It is a day marked in celebration of one's ancestors, with offerings and rituals held in their honor.

<u>Yule</u>: Held on the Winter Solstice, around the 21st of December, Yule is the day on which the Goddess gives birth to the Sun God. It is typically celebrated as a day of positivity, with fire-related rituals to symbolize rebirth and energy. It represents life, hope, and warmth.

<u>Imbolc</u>: Usually held around the beginning of February, Imbolc is another seasonal celebration which marks the beginning of Spring. It celebrates the nurturing of the growing God's strength upon the bosom of the Goddess. This day is representative of healing, purification and inspiration, and is a good time for initiations – either into Wicca as an individual practitioner or into a coven.

<u>Ostara</u>: This is the celebration of the Summer Equinox, and marks the day when the God and Goddess begin their celestial courtship. It is a day of new beginnings upon which Wiccans contemplate on their hope and dreams for the future, typically celebrated around the 21st of March.

Beltain: This day is celebrated at the beginning of May, and marks the day when the Lord and Goddess consummate their relationship. This day is celebrated as a representation of fertility, and for appreciation of everything that Wiccans have already achieved in life. It is a period of growth of wisdom, and contemplation in gratitude to found love or commitment. It marks the half-way period through the Wheel of the Year.

Litha: This celebration is held on the Summer Solstice, and marks a period where the Goddess is pregnant with the God. This is the point where the Sun Lord is at his peak strength, before his decline and eventual death on Samhain. It is held as a day of peak magical power, and is a celebration of abundance and bounty. It is usually celebrated around the 21st of June.

Lughnasadh: This day is marked by a feast to the Earth Mother, and celebrates the entire cycle of life, harvest and death. It is typically celebrated around the 1st of August, and marks the celebration of the first harvest. This day is marked as a day of deliverance for wishes which were meditated upon in previous Sabbats, and so rituals will be oriented towards ripening and harvesting wishes.

Mabon: Mabon is the last Sabbat before Samhain when the entire cycle starts again, and marks the Autumn Equinox. It is typically held around the 22nd of September, and is representative of the phase where the God has developed in the womb of the Goddess and is now awaiting (re)birth after the death of his previous year's form on Samhain. It is a day of contemplation upon the past year, and a celebration in gratitude of everything which has been achieved due to the efforts of this past year. It is the point in the year where darkness slowly starts overtaking the light, marking the cycle to death for the Lord.

Each of these days mark a major celebration for Wiccans, and are typically held with multiple covens meeting at designated locations for mass rituals. The rituals held for each day differ strongly from one another in meaning and constituent material. If you wish to perform these rituals by yourself, there is an overwhelmingly large amount of source material on the internet for the same. If you also wish to celebrate each Esbat, there are rites for the full moon which you may acquire from the internet, depending on your reasons for the rituals and the needs which you wish fulfilled through each, or else you may use the knowledge from the subsequent chapters to frame your own spell.

Chapter 5: Choosing Your Mystical Name

Before we move on to the odds and ends of your Wicca practice, the first thing you need to do is to contemplate on your mystical name. While all of us are given a name upon birth, Wicca believes that names have great power over an individual object or being. As such, we also believe that each of us has a deeper mystical name which describes the essence of our being, and which we alone can determine for ourselves.

Traditionally, a witch researches and decides on a name in the first year of practice, and only assumes that name after a year and one day from initiation into Wicca. Not only does this mark an auspicious period which lets you wash your personality of anything which you would wish to purify yourself from, but also allows you to give this process the respect which it deserves. The biggest mistake which you could make would be to choose a name simply because it sounds "cool". You aren't choosing a screen name here, and the extent to which you can correctly determine your own mystical name will greatly affect your success in spells where naming yourself plays a big part in identification.

You may feel the need to change your name once or twice in your life, as and when you feel that your personality has changed enough for the older name to no longer apply to you – but changing your name frequently will mark you as a joke among other Wiccans. If you wish to dedicate your inner being to a deity, do not choose their name – but rather form a derivative which would allow you to pay tribute to their essence without encroaching on the territory of their power. As I mentioned, names have power, and taking the name of a deity is plainly insulting and arrogant beyond belief.

Some people also choose two names, one which is only known to themselves and the other which is only known to their coven mates and is used in group rituals. This allows Wiccans to preserve the innermost essence of their being within themselves, while revealing sufficiently enough of that essence to ensure success in group rituals.

Chapter 6: The Book of Shadows, Altar Tools, and Herbalism

[A] The Book of Shadows

A witch's Book of Shadows (BoS) is his/her *everything*. It is the essence of their devotion and dedication to their chosen deity, and the tome which holds all their spells and rituals. The BoS begins with every bit of research and mythology which you can unearth about your chosen deity, as well as any poetry or art work in their honor, and marks the extent of your dedication to their service. It also contains your almanac marking important dates, as well as your mystical name (if you choose to keep one that's just for yourself). Since energy is the basis of power, everything in the BoS is written by hand – which imbues energy into your book and elevates its status to your most crucial tool. It is vital that no one else open your BoS or even look through it without your permission. If you wish to share it with your HP or HPS, you should grant them permission beforehand, and only allow perusal of such parts which you deem appropriate.

Your BoS also contains any laws or regulations which you wish to abide by, and the act of your writing them down is symbolic of you agreeing to spiritually abide by the limitations which you've set upon yourself. These laws may either be your own, or those of your coven. It should also contain your research on stones, herbs, crystals and other symbols, and your own understanding of the power of each.

The BoS is also the repository of your entire arcana – rites, rituals, spells, major religious experiences, spiritual dreams, etc. It should contain the essence of your entire spiritual being, and be a chronicle of every major point in your religious undertaking. Over the course of a lifetime, you may need to change your BoS a few times, and keep upgrading to larger binders or diaries. Make sure that you note everything down again by hand each time, so as to transfer your imbued spiritual energy from one book to another, and offer up your older book to your deity by disposing of it only in running water (rivers, ocean, etc.) or by burning it in a fire.

[B] Basic Altar Tools

The basic altar tools which every Wiccan needs are:

Pentacle – A five-point star which is a powerful symbol of protection and thus is placed in the very centre of the altar.

Cup or Chalice – An altar chalice is usually kept in the direction of Water –West– and is used to hold ceremonial drinks during rituals. Chalices hold goddess energy, and silver ones work especially well given their nature.

Athame – a double-bladed ritualistic knife, may be metal or wood. It holds male god energy, and is used to focus and direct energies in a ritual. It shouldn't be used on any other physical activity.

Bell – Esoteric traditions such as Buddhism have long held the ability of bells to cleanse the energies in an environment. A bell's sound, when you're purchasing it, should personally appeal to you and call forth a bond to it from within you. Take your time to search for a bell which uplifts you through its tone.

Representation – This refers to any representation, idol or image of your chosen deity. Wiccans believe that these representations may hold some of the god or goddess' actual energy within them after adequate devotion and dedication, and so are treated accordingly with the utmost reverence.

Offering Dish – This is typically a bowl or dish which is specifically used to provide offerings to your deity. Once the ritual is over, you can either burn the offerings or pour them specifically into running natural waters (rivers, oceans, etc.)

Candles – Candles are often color-coded and used in specific directions. Black, green or brown candles are typically placed in the north; white ones in the East; Red or orange ones in the south; blue ones in the west; silver candles for the goddess in the centre, and gold ones for gods in the same position. These are used to call upon the powers of each direction, and provide a point of focus for each. Apart from these color-coded ones, you may find specific candles for particular gods and goddesses as well. Never re-use a candle for a fresh ritual or spell, or even a prayer – since it's believed that a candle, once lit, absorbs impure energies from the environment. Always make sure that you light an unused candle. There are also several rituals which need candles that last for multiple days, or which can't be completed till the candle burns out on its own – so make sure you always do your homework, and choose the best candle for the process. If you wish to avoid wastage, don't reuse a candle but instead melt it down and cast a new one from a half-used piece. Make sure to purify the wax with a tiny amount of salt or light purifying herbs while remaking the new candle.

Incenses, Stones & Crystals – Different colored stones have differing meaning and symbolic functions. Extensive research on the same is easily found through quick searches online. For some Wiccans, especially those who may have chosen to dedicate themselves to Nordic deities, stones with runic sigils carved into them function more effectively than crystals. Since rituals heavily derive their power and energy from associated symbols, the closer you can get to providing all the associated elements of your deity in each ritual, the more success you're likely to observe in your endeavors.

As always, since Wicca is a spiritual path of resonance with energy, pay careful attention to your choice of altar tools. While each tool has a specific purpose, any similar article can fulfill its need in a ritual as well – so use those articles which call out to you the strongest.

[C] Herbs and Plants

Herbalism and witchcraft have had a long history together, with some of the first medicine men and women being herbalist druids and witches who studied the spiritual and physiological effects of plants on the human body, and so made use of them on both levels to help those in need. While some herbs are burnt at the altar, others are burnt before to purify the environment, while others still are consumed (be very careful with herbs that you consume, since some may be extremely toxic; always do your research thoroughly before consuming any herb, and if in doubt, avoid that element altogether till you can corroborate your knowledge with more experienced practitioners or botanists).

Some common examples are – valerian for anxiety; rosemary or catnip for beauty; cinnamon and yarrow for courage; honeysuckle for depression; bay leaf for employment opportunities or professional achievement; vanilla for friendship; sage for intuition; hickory for justice or legal issues; lavender for love; sandalwood for protection; jasmine for prophecy; oak for strength; hazel for wisdom, etc.

Chapter 7:   Conducting 4-Step
Spellcraft

As intimidating as it may seem, creating your own spells is an extremely easy process. Of course, you will likely need to learn to do a bit of tweaking through trial-and-error before you're able to effectively perform a new spell, but don't let that hold you back in any way. Each time you make some headway, the rush which you'll feel from the heady implications of success will offset anything else you may have to go through, including the occasional repetition in efforts sometimes. Always keep in mind that Wiccan spell casting is a transfer of energy from you and your surroundings into a pre-determined and focused outcome, as directed by your will. The essential part here is that you be emotionally and spiritually focused upon realizing your outcome – so much so that you should be able to visualize it with absolute clarity in your mind. Once you attain such a focused state, which isn't difficult to do after an hour of practice for most beginners, you should be able to feel the flow of energy in the spell as well as the uplifting joy if it's successful.

To create your own spell, you need to first have a very specific goal in mind. Just simply wishing "Let me do better at work" isn't enough because it's too vague and relies on too many elements to go smoothly. Instead, concentrate on "Let my boss like me better" or "Let my day go smoothly tomorrow" or "Let me finish my work the fastest out of all my colleagues tomorrow" for example – the more specific your need, the better.

Once you've identified your need, break it down into its basic constituents. Which god or goddess do you wish to summon? Athena for wisdom? The celtic Tailtiu for vigor and endurance? After you've decided on the deity, complete your research on him/her as thoroughly as you can to identify symbols and key arcane ingredients – is there an animal associated with, or are there any colors or plants linked to the deity? Are there any symbols, hieroglyphs, sigils or runes which describe or depict your chosen deity? You already know the basic altar setup, and your research should tell you which colors, crystals or stones you should concentrate on apart from symbols associated with the deity.

After you've identified the key components, start writing your spell. The simplest way to do this is through these 4 simple steps:

[1] First sentence invokes the grace of the deity, and involves providing any favorable offering or incense smoke.

[2] Second sentence spells out the exact nature of your need.

[3] Third sentence invites the power of the deity into you, coupled with burning or consuming (if non-toxic or non-allergenic) any ingredient associated with that purpose.

[4] Fourth sentence shows your gratitude to the deity, and gives thanks for his/her attention towards you.

This is just one way of going about this process, and you can modify this procedure anyway that feels right to you. Just make sure that your spell rhymes. This isn't for some childish need to stick to one format. Rather, it has been proven that rhyming allows for rhythmic chanting which allows one to focus on the task at hand without needing to get too lost in the words themselves. Remember that energy transfer here is an emotional and spiritual process, not a public speech or competition of eloquence. If you write the most moving poem on the planet, yet feel as dead as a dodo inside, the spell is going to remain a bust.

As a simple start, to provide you with some beginner's experience, I'm also listing some basic spells here.

Calming Spell

This spell has helped me disperse any emotional upheaval at various points in my past, and is the perfect spell for a beginner. It can be cast with a candle, a blue-colored crystal or a stone. What you need to do is first wet a little bit of basil and place a single leaf in your mouth. Hold it there and don't chew or swallow. If you're using a crystal, make sure to keep a bowl full of salt water nearby. Hold the crystal between your hands, and close your eyes. Concentrate on the basil in your mouth and start chewing. As soon as you swallow, focus all that turbulence and turmoil and envision it flowing into the crystal, disappearing endlessly into the blue depth.

Along with it, chant the following:

Masters of the West,

Keepers of Sea and Ocean,

Disperse the Unrest,

Smite the unruly emotion.

As I will it, fulfill my devotion.

Once you calm down, and feel the emotional tide dissipate, put the crystal in the salt water and leave it be for a while. After some time, wash it thoroughly and store it properly again.

If you're outside and unable to use any of the paraphernalia – simply pick up a stone and clasp it between your hands. Envision the emotions pour endlessly into the stone, and repeat the chant. Once you're done and feel calmer, throw the stone away.

Spell to Dispel Fear

I've had a few moments in my life when I was immensely afraid to take a certain step, though I knew it was the correct choice to make. It was my own fear which was holding me back, the constant worry of the unknown or fear of a big risk backfiring. This is a pretty simple spell in such times, and will give you the courage to take a step forward when you most need it.

What you need for this is a small handkerchief, a sprig of sage, three acorns, three cinnamon quills, two pieces of paper, and a mason jar.

Put salt water in the Mason jar and leave it at your altar with some purifying sage smoldering around it. After the water has been purified, write your biggest source of courage, as well as the outcome which you fear the most on two separate pieces of paper. Put the cinnamon and acorns in the handkerchief and tie it into a small bundle. Put the paper containing your fear into the water, and close the jar. Put the jar in the freezer. Now sit at the altar, and burn the paper with the outcome you hope for the most while praying to your deity.

Chant the following:

Fears frozen,

Hope offered,

In this time of courage,

Devotion proffered,

Path chosen,

Destiny fixed,

Guidance requested

For troubles amidst.

While you're chanting this, visualize the feared outcome being trapped in the creeping ice, while your hope rises to the deities on the spiritual energy of your devotion and strength. Imagine the hopes being received by your deity who – smiling upon you – transfers you the strength needed to make your hopes come to fruition in the small bundle. Once you're done, keep that bundle in your pocket and carry it with you whether awake or asleep 'til your hopes come to fruition. Whenever you feel fearful or worried again, concentrate on the bundle – now a buzzing mass of energy – and visualize a stream of energy transferring from it to you. If you need to, you can also just visualize the frozen and impotent fear sitting in your freezer. After a few hours of it being frozen, dispose of it in some running water (or some lake or pond nearby).

This spell may also have an unintended effect on your dreams. Twice in my life, after casting this spell, I got a dream on the same night which showed me a solution that seemed too foolhardy and risky to work. However, upon trying it, the outcome was even better than I had originally planned for. If you receive a similar dream, don't reject it out of hand – seriously consider giving it a shot since it may be guidance from your deity.

Conclusion

Witches are a vastly misunderstood people in general, and a vastly twisted image in popular perception. It could happen that you face some opposition in your goals to follow Wicca as your chosen religion. However, never lie in such a situation – rather, attempt to educate the people opposing you if they're close enough to you that you may need their support in the future. This may particularly hold true for your parents. But remember that nothing good can start with a lie.

Never attempt to make fun of your own religious beliefs, or denigrate it by threatening to curse another just because they've been singling you out or persecuting you because of your religious beliefs. The Wiccan community is far larger than you are, and such instances only serve to deepen the mainstream bias and ridicule that they face from time to time. I've alternately spent vast amounts of time with some covens, and practicing by myself – and both experiences bring with them unique joys. So never get too hung up on one or the other.

Always keep in mind the primary rule of Wicca – never unduly harm another. Apart from this, you're pretty much free to do as you please, as long as you keep the three-fold law in mind.

Welcome, Brother or Sister, to the world of the Wiccae. May your journey soar like an eagle's on a warm wind, and bring with it unbound love and joy.

Finally, I'd like to thank you for purchasing this book! If you enjoyed it or found it helpful, I'd greatly appreciate it if you'd take a moment to leave a review on Amazon. Thank you!

Printed in Great Britain
by Amazon

12415113R00041